MY YEAR ON THE FARM

Memories of Grandma Isabella

BRIAN J. SMITH

AuthorHouse™ LLC
1663 Liberty Drive
Bloomington, IN 47403
www.authorhouse.com
Phone: 1-800-839-8640

Published by AuthorHouse 12/18/2013

ISBN: 978-1-4918-4058-0 (sc)
*   978-1-4918-4059-7 (e)*

Library of Congress Control Number: 2013923112

Any people depicted in stock imagery provided by Thinkstock are models,
and such images are being used for illustrative purposes only.
Certain stock imagery © Thinkstock.

This book is printed on acid-free paper.

authorHOUSE®

Preface

Lately I've had recurring dreams about things that happened nearly 50 years ago. Memories that are imbued with a warm glow of nostalgia for a time that has long passed. Inevitably, these memories center around "the farm". Specifically, it was grandma's farm and my family were just visitors on weekends and holidays until we came to live there for a year.

My childhood is divided into two main locations; nine years growing up in a suburb of the City of Sarnia, Ontario, then eight years living in the small town of Ingersoll. However, in between these two settings is the one year I lived on grandma's dairy farm. The experiences I had on the farm are so different from suburban and town life that it has obviously left a lasting impression on me.

At age nine, I was old enough to be free to find my own adventures without constant adult supervision, yet not old enough to be tied down with daily laborious responsibilities. I could choose to go for a walk in the woods with the dog, or fetch bales of hay to feed the cows if asked. Freedom in a wide-open space with open fields stretching to the horizon instead of feeling closed in by buildings.

The time on the farm was also the end of an era. Times were changing rapidly. The wood stove and horses would be replaced. Very few farmers raise pigs and cows side by side anymore. Television and telephone systems were archaic by today's standards. The entire concept of a family dairy farm has largely disappeared and transformed into a corporate enterprise where hourly shift workers arrive and conduct the milking tasks for herds as large as 500, like my distant Heeney cousins near Centerville.

I undertook the writing of this book to honour the memories of my grandmother. Her entire life can be divided into three main parts; her childhood growing up on a farm near Ingersoll, her marriage to Frank Heeney and raising two children in the 1930's and 1940's and finally her years on the Brock Wilson farm. She spent 99 percent of her life in a ten mile radius from her burial place at Harris Street Cemetery. She worked constantly.

More than her example of industriousness was her quiet competence as a farm manager and wise and loving grandmother.

I started this project thinking I would research a thorough history of my grandmother's life, then found this to be unmanageable. Then, I thought I'd concentrate on the year at the farm with anecdotes regarding everyone who lived there at the time. This was more manageable, but my memories and interpretation of events concerning my parents and siblings might differ markedly from what they witnessed. It seemed presumptuous of me to tell other people's stories. In the end I concentrated only on events that I could recollect with some analysis of their meaning.

What I hope this book provides is a little historical context of farm life in rural Ontario in the 1960's. The era of the 1960's starts with black and white images and ends in a swirling kaleidoscope of colour. From unison mop-top Beatles singing "I Want to Hold Your Hand" to their frenetic screaming in "Helter Skelter". From Innocence to Experience. The year 1967 seems to be a transition between these extremes. My memories of farm life in 1967 include the image of our horses pulling a hay rake to the singing of modern patriotic jingles in the classroom.

Finally, I wrote the book so that my own grandchildren could have some understanding of my own childhood. I would love to have had the opportunity to find out about my own great-great grandfather's 1830 childhood in Ireland. However, my ancestors experiences are lost to the sands of time. Perhaps in the year 2067 when I'm long gone, my grandchildren will visit the laneway where the farm once stood and think of their grandfather as a child who once skipped and sang songs down the very same laneway as he greeted a new summer and new life on the farm.

THE YEAR ON THE FARM

Even now, when I look at the picture 43 years later, I'm amused by the fact that she's the only one wearing a sensible hat in the hot Florida sun. That's Grandma in the middle with the long overcoat and the stoic, George Washington smile. Sister Brenda is on the left, arms folded and a couple of steps away from Mom, perhaps impatient to get on with this excursion. Next is my mother, Noreen in a striped pant suit and sunglasses that gave her a rather feline look. My father, Jack, is beside me holding binoculars at a time when his hair was as dark as his sunglasses. Finally, that's me on the right at age 13 trying hard to look cool and not too much like the tourist that I was. Missing from the picture is brother Phil, who was home in Ingersoll that Christmas. This picture is one of a very few that exist of my grandmother. The six of us lived together on the farm from the summer of 1966 to the summer of 1967.

The picture was taken December 29, 1970 on the gangplank of a tourist boat that would take us around the canals and lagoons of Fort Lauderdale. We would marvel at the magnificent homes which had a large car parked out front and a yacht tied to the dock out back. This was wealth and luxury none of us had ever known. I wonder what was going through grandma's mind as we cruised through this exotic landscape. She had only known a lifetime of hard work and adherence to her Baptist faith. I remember she had caught a cold on the long drive down to Florida and this cold lingered into a debilitating sinus infection or perhaps pneumonia. In just five weeks after this picture was taken, she would be dead.

Isabella Ancestry

Grandma is Isabelle Wilson. She was born Isabella Thomas and raised on a farm just a short distance from the present day Elm Hurst Inn in West Oxford Township. She once told me her father's ancestors were "United Empire Loyalists" - the pro-British monarchists forced out of the United States in the late 1700's who joined Thomas Ingersoll in his quest to forge a new settlement in the wilderness of West Canada. There is Irish blood on her mother's side from County Armagh in the Emerald Isle. She was the third of six sisters and one brother; Margaret (Blackman 1897 - 1923), Edith (Hargreaves 1899 - 1952), Isabella (Heeney / Wilson 1903 - 1971), Phoebe (Powell 1908 - 1996), Gladys (McMurray 1911 - 1995), and twins Jean (Nancekivell 1915 - 1995) and Bill (1915 - 1968).

I once asked her how far she got in school and she told me grade six - which was rather typical of farm girls back then. There certainly was a lot of work to do on a family farm, and she certainly learned the difficult challenge of operating a fully self-sufficient organic farm. When she was a child, the Prime Minister was Sir Wilfrid Laurier. I recall asking her if she knew anything about him. She said that she could remember the time when he was our leader and that he was a "catch cold". Not knowing what that meant, she explained to me that people thought that Laurier was an illegitimate child born out of wedlock. Closer research implies that Laurier probably fathered an illegitimate child while in office rather than being one. Maybe she meant to say Laurier *fathered* a "catch cold". Interesting phrase though; "catch cold."

A typical farm circa 1900

Frank Heeney

Isabella married Frank Heeney, my grandfather, in nearby Salford in 1928. Frank was a Great War veteran 19 years older than Isabel who managed the small family farm outside Ingersoll. The farm was named Vimy Ridge as a tribute to his participation in the great victory on the battlefield in 1917. Together they had two children; Noreen (born 1929) and Terry (born 1930). Frank was known as someone who liked to tease and tell jokes. For instance Terry's full name is Patrick Terrence Heeney. Apparently he used to make jokes about an Irish stock character "Paddy", prompting a perturbed Isabel to begin calling her son Terry instead of Patrick. Frank was injured twice during the Great War and was known to run for cover when he heard blasting at the Beachville limestone quarry pits. He put his faith in horses as a mode of transportation and never learned to drive a car. Perhaps he saw enough of mechanized death on the Western Front to distrust automobiles. He was a proud man who refused a government military pension even though he was certainly eligible for one due to his service in World War One. Frank passed away in 1953 at age 69 when Isabel was 50 years old.

The Heeney family circa 1933: Frank, Terry, Isabella, Noreen with Uncle Fred Heeney

Challenges

I once asked grandma what life was like in the 1930's. She looked away with a far-off look in her eye and said, "It was a very tough time...they came to call it the 'dirty thirties'". It was a time when the price of everything dropped so low that it often cost more to feed and raise livestock than to sell it. Farmers grew large vegetable gardens and kept their produce in basement sand cellars to eat year-round. Canning preserves was vital for survival. Unemployed beggars called "hobos" roamed the countryside looking for work.

"The worst day of my life was when Donny Blackman died". She was referring to her 11 year-old nephew Donny Blackman who drowned at Port Burwell beach during a rare family outing on July 1st 1931. One imagines Isabella frantically searching the crashing waves of Lake Erie with two little toddlers in her arms. Donny's mother was Aunt Alice, who I remember as a tiny, serious woman always dressed in black. Alice lived her life in an apartment on Aunt Gladys' property beside the Harris Street Cemetery.

Tombstone of grandma's sister May, brother-in-law Harry, second wife Alice, and
Donny, who drowned July 1st, 1931

Grandma getting set to drive to Ingersoll in the days before her Oldsmobile Delta 88

The War Years

    The early 1940's saw War return to Canada as the British Empire fought Adolph Hitler's Nazis. This meant rationing of certain commodities such as sugar and gasoline. However, markets for farm produce increased and a certain amount of prosperity was possible with a lot of hard work. The herd of milking cows gradually increased from a dozen to over twenty. Isabella and Frank were raising two young teenagers; Noreen and Terry. Journal entries from Noreen indicate that Frank was sick a lot. On February 10, 1945, Isabella "shovelled snow all afternoon so we can get horses up to Canan road. Snow terrible deep". Much of the diary documents the seasonal rhythm of the farm from ploughing, seeding, hoeing, raking, thrashing, cutting and harvesting crops. Nearly all of it done the horse-drawn way. The entire family participated in daily milking chores where each person was responsible for hand-milking a few cows. At the end of August, 1944, the family house and barn was wired for electricity.

    Education for her children was a high priority for Isabella. Both Noreen and Terry were excellent students. Noreen went on to graduate from Woodstock Nursing College in 1950, at a time when careers for women were rather limited. Terry went on to earn a Bachelor of Arts degree from McMaster University and eventually became Principal at Dutton elementary school.

Brock Wilson

Isabella's first husband, Frank Heeney passed away in April 1953 from complications related to chronic bleeding ulcers. Shortly thereafter, Isabella sold the farm with all livestock and implements at auction. Every cow that was up for auction had "Vime" in it's name as a reference to Vimy Ridge. She remained a widow for three years then married Brock Banbury Wilson on May 15, 1956. Brock was a bachelor farmer who had lived at the farm with his sister and family for many years. He was over 60 years old when he married grandma. He had known Isabella for his whole life as she lived just one country road over from him. Together, Brock and Isabella honeymooned to Western Canada and U.S.A. in the summer of 1956. Isabella made a scrapbook of their journey with postcards and captions. A portion of this scrapbook still exists.

Brock Wilson, Grandma Isabella and Aunt Alice Blackman with Phillip and me out front.

My memories of Brock are short and fleeting. It is the summer of 1962. I'm 5 years old and about to start Kindergarten. Brock is a rather quiet, shy, kindly, reserved old man. He is seated on a chair beside the kitchen wood stove near the door of the woodshed. His feet are in a bucket and grandma is pouring warm water into the bucket. Perhaps Brock is suffering from gout or some other ailment that makes his feet very sore and soaking them in warm water brings some relief. My other memory of Brock is Christmas 1962. Our family was driving from our home in Sarnia to the homestead and our car got stuck in the snow about a half mile from the farm. A short time passes with dad spinning the tires deeper into the snow and someone arrives on a tractor to pull us out of the snow bank. It is Brock who is driving the tractor. He attaches a chain to our car and pulls us to the sanctuary of the warm farmhouse.

Brock died in January of 1963. His funeral is my very first experience with death. The funeral home was located on Duke Street in Ingersoll. I recall with confused fascination seeing his dead body in the open casket. I had to keep quiet and not fidget while the minister did the talking. Something like church without the exit to Sunday School.

Hiking the Countryside

The Wilson farm that grandma inherited was located on the second concession out of the town of Ingersoll (R. R. #4) about a mile from Highway 19 and two miles from Culloden Road. It was about a half mile up from the railway tracks. The homestead and barn were surrounded on all sides by fields that provided crops to feed the cattle. In the northwest corner is a woodland situated right beside the railway tracks.

My earliest memory of exploring the local countryside comes from a hike with my uncle Terry and cousins Janice and Donald in the summer of 1964. We walked down the lane behind the barn, past the large rock pile and apple tree then hopped the fence onto Curry Way's property. Terry helped us three kids up the toboggan hill and over the next field as we came upon S. S. #2 Dereham elementary school. This was the school both Terry and Noreen attended back in the 1940's. It was closing down as a school that summer, but we were able to enter as it was unlocked. Old desks with holes for inkwells were stacked to one side as the building was getting prepared for auction. Terry stepped out and looked out across the train tracks to his old homestead birthplace that his parents had worked.

Donald and uncle Terry Heeney, 1964

Uncle Terry, Donald, Janice and me at the farm getting ready to hike the countryside.

We made our way East and eventually ended up at Aunt Glady's house. Isabelle's sister Gladys was a very friendly woman with an infectious hearty laugh. She was also very good at sign language as her husband, Merton, was deaf. If one was having a conversation with Gladys and Merton was nearby, she would instinctively give a quick hand-sign translation for him to keep in the conversation. Her farmstead was located across the field from Harris Street cemetery where many of the Thomas, Heeney and Wilson ancestors are buried. In 1964, her farm was still probably a viable milking operation before it was all sold off to Currie Way. I know things got tough for her financially in later life as she took a job processing turkeys at Checkerboard Farms well into her 60's. After a short visit, Terry and us kids all hiked back to the Wilson homestead through the open fields.

The Farmhouse

Even though the farmhouse had a formal front door and large porch facing the road, this entrance was very rarely used. We always came in the back door from the barn. Under the back steps was a straw bed where the collie dog, Cindy stayed. Soon after entering, there was a large washbasin where there would be occasional line ups of working men during haying time. The kitchen was the hub of activity and always had a warm smell from the wood-burning stove. After the kitchen was the dining room that had a large table that could seat about 15 people at Christmas time. The television was rather new at this time and was in the corner of the dining room that could be viewed from a couch. In keeping with Victorian tradition, the parlour was always kept in tidy shape and had an unused fire place, carpeting, cactus collection and a piano. A curious romantic painting of a sleepy young girl and a protective large dog stared down at us from the wall. Off the parlour was a desk for the telephone and a large staircase with a banister that was fun to slide down to the landing.

The farmhouse was a great place to play hide-and-seek. I recall playing this with my sister Brenda and the house was so big for children that one of the rules we made for the game was for us to only hide upstairs because using the whole house took so long to find someone. There were five bedrooms and one bathroom upstairs. The room facing the barn was for the hired hand. At the top of the stairs to the right was a small room where my brother and I slept in bunk beds. Brenda's room was down across the hall. My parents took the room at the end of the hall across from grandma's master bedroom. I recall hiding in grandma's closet during one game of hide-and-seek and marvelling at all the nice clothes and a small sitting desk with a hair brush. Since I really only knew grandma with her gnarled work hands and work clothes, the image of her sitting at a mirror and brushing her hair seemed entirely out of character.

The Farm

Aerial Photo of Farm

The farm as it looked in 1961
Photo courtesy of Susanne Wilson

10

Laneway from Farmhouse to Road / Girl and Dog picture from the parlour

Delta 88

Another memory from the summer of 1964 was when grandma took me and the cousins to town in her 1956 Oldsmobile. This car was designed way before seatbelts were mandatory and only had a rope slung atop the front bench seat to hang onto for safety. In the back seat was Donald and Brenda, age 5, Janice 6, and senior me at age 7. Grandma was a careful, slow driver so we didn't need to hold onto the rope very hard. When we got to Ingersoll, we all piled into the Metropolitan Department store where grandma picked up a few things then shepherded us kids back into the Olds for the trip back home.

A couple of years later, grandma went shopping to replace the '56 Olds with a newer model. Danny Dunlop was the car salesman she dealt with at Fleischer and Jewett motors. The most important thing that she was looking for in a new car was ample trunk space. "I need it wide and deep enough to carry a calf." Grandma often took newborn calves to cattle auction in Norwich and could save a lot of transport fees if she took the calf to auction herself. It didn't really matter that the new 1966 Delta 88 Olds had power steering, power windows or a V8 engine...it had to have enough trunk space to carry a calf!

Beatles

At age seven, my head just barely cleared the dining room table, but something happened there in the summer of 1964 that probably ignited my passion for music. The hired hand, Henry Vergeer, took all of a week's wages and bought a portable record player and one album. The album was "Twist and Shout" by the Beatles. The cover showed the four lads from Liverpool in their grey suits and Beatle boots jumping in unison. Henry set up the record player on the dining room table and played his record whenever he could. The infectious music wasn't anything like I had ever heard before since I was brought up on a musical diet of George Beverly Shea and Perry Como. This music made me move! To this day whenever I hear early Beatles songs such as "Boys", "Chains", "She Loves You" and "Twist and Shout" - I think of the dining room table and this incredible music wafting through the country pastures of the farm. I would later make an entire career as a music teacher and attribute that album as ground zero for my passion in everything Beatles and popular music.

I recently did a bit of research on this particular album and found it was manufactured in Canada under the Rainbow label. You couldn't buy this particular album in the USA or England. It features John Lennon singing lead on four songs, Paul McCartney and George Harrison with two each, Lennon / McCartney sharing four, with Ringo singing one. This confirms my suspicion that it was indeed John Lennon who was the most influential Beatle in the very early days of their fame. Later Beatles albums from 1967 onwards would show Paul McCartney as having a stronger influence.

Beatles were very big in 1964
Bigger than the Thomas Picnic

Thomas Picnic

    One weekend in the summer of 1964, our family joined grandma and over 50 other people for the 54th annual Thomas Family Reunion picnic. All of grandma's siblings and relatives gathered at Southside Park in Woodstock for an afternoon of fun and games and delicious home cooked meals. I recall purchasing some Beatles cards there for 5 cents where you would get four cards and a stick of gum. This event was important enough that it merited a column in the Woodstock Sentinel Review newspaper where I apparently won a foot race against other kids my age. The last Thomas family Reunion picnic was held in Memorial Park, Ingersoll in the summer of 1967 shortly before uncle Bill Thomas died. He was the last in the line to carry the Thomas name as he was the only boy with six sisters, grandma included.

Claude

Claude Banbury is someone I met around this time (1964). His mother, Pearl, was very good friends with grandma and possibly related to Brock "Banbury" Wilson. His father John was killed by a car in 1965 right in front of his house when he stepped out onto the highway to fetch the mail. Claude was a classmate of my mother. After Brock died, I think he dropped by the farm house to help grandma as much as he could. I have an early memory of sitting on his knee in grandma's kitchen dunking my cookie into his coffee. He would drive grandma to Sarnia for visits. I recall him joking with my parents about the red Lester B Pearson election sign in front of our house. My parents often voted Liberal, but Claude pretended to be bothered by this and pulled out the red sign and pleaded with them to replace it with the Conservative blue sign of John Diefenbaker. I also recall Claude being at my first piano recital in Sarnia where I played "Big Chief Thundercloud". This piece of music with its repetitive war chant pounding probably did little to advance sensitivity to Aboriginal issues. On another occasion, Claude surprised me by appearing at the gate of my school and walking me home. He was this friendly man who often drove Grandma to Sarnia in his green Impala car and was often at the farm.

Even though Claude was about 40 years old at the time, he was balding on top and combed over the long hair on the side of his head to hide his baldness. He wore glasses and had a set of false teeth. He lived with his parents and his brother Rich on a farm across the fields on #19 highway that you could see from grandma's farm. The barn was unkempt and very dirty and parts of it seemed to be falling apart. A gaggle of hissing geese roamed around the barnyard. When I came upon a goose egg, I was known to smack it up against the barn wall to hear it pop. Claude could care less if we lost a goose egg. A seething bull cow was once contained in a small stall inside the barn and it butted the walls so hard the entire barn shook.

Powder

Claude and I once exploded a mix of powders on his farm. I was there when we went to the Ingersoll pharmacy to buy a package of potash, then some sulphur. The pharmacist was Mr. McDougall and he seemed very reluctant to sell the two powders to us, asking what we wanted to do with it. Anyway, he sold the powders to us and we went back to the Banbury Farm. On a flat surface next to a retaining wall, we carefully poured out the yellow potash and topped it off with the sulphur powder. We then climbed to the top of the wall and dropped a large rock onto the powder. It did indeed produce a huge bang of an explosion! I guess farmers knew about what these powders could do, and we just wanted to cause this explosion for kicks!

Spock

Although the barn was dirty and messy, the farmhouse was neat and tidy as his mother Pearl tended the housework. Pearl was never in the barnyard doing chores the way my grandma always did. She had something wrong with her back or hips and walked with a slow painful limp. Occasionally I was at their house for dinner and recall eating "home fried" potatoes for the very first time. There was a huge collection of antique clocks in the front room and Claude and I would wind them all up to one minute to 12 - then listen to the clanging din as all twelve clocks chimed together. I recall watching television at his house when this eerie theme music came on. It featured a strange character named "Spock" who had pointed ears and talked in a deadpan manner. This was probably the very first broadcast of Star Trek and I was there to witness it. Unfortunately at the time, I just thought the show too strange for me and did not become a fan. The original t.v. show only lasted three seasons.

Rich

He and Rich did not get along at all. Rich was rather grouchy all the time and pretty much pretended that I wasn't even there. I would sometimes go help Claude with the milking chores at his farm by fetching the cows from pasture and we would find Rich curled up in a ball laying on the floor of the barn sound asleep. It turned out he was a drunkard. Claude was very frustrated at having to do pretty much all the farm chores himself, but had to share the meagre proceeds from farming with his brother.

Since Claude was such a reluctant farmer, he took on an additional job as a solo house painter in the afternoons. He often wore overalls with paint splattered all over them. During the day when he wasn't painting, he would take me with him to Woodstock to purchase paint and to visit customer's houses to lay down tarp and position ladders to prepare the site for painting. One of the sites was a church in the village of Zenda and I sat and played little songs on the church organ while he worked. In the evening, after chores, Claude took me to all kinds of places such as the Nilestown Speedway, where I saw car races and "demolition derbies" for the first time. I came to know the Ingersoll Dairy Freeze on the outskirts of town where he would buy me ice cream cones or milkshakes - whatever I wanted! We often played miniature golf at a place in Beachville. Claude was a lonely bachelor who never found a woman to share his life, but seemed to enjoy the company of an eight year-old boy. I think other people and family members thought that it was rather strange that he was often hanging around with a young child. I look back on him as a person who was very nice to me, treated me well and offered experiences that educators would call "enrichment". I only saw Claude on two occasions after grandma passed away. Once, right after her funeral, and another chance encounter while I was working after school at Walker's Furniture. Otherwise, he faded completely from my life after I left the farm. Just lately, I found out he died in 1998, but I never heard of his passing at the time.

Moving

Our family moved to the farm in the summer of 1966 for two reasons. First, my father, Jack, had been accepted to the University of Western Ontario in London to begin studies to become a minister. Secondly, grandma was running a large dairy operation by herself with the help of hired hands and could use some assistance from our family. I had heard reports of grandma coming down with a bad case of "shingles" in the spring of 1966. Shingles in adults is a very painful outbreak of chicken pox that is often brought about by stress and worry. Farmers are continually under stress from the weather and health of livestock and as agricultural practices became more modern in the 1960's, keeping a family dairy operation solvent became an increasingly arduous challenge.

Jack

My father, William John Smith, had a particularly difficult childhood. Stricken with rickets as a toddler, he couldn't walk until age 5 and had to be carried everywhere. His mother died in childbirth when Jack was only six. His family of six children struggled through the Great Depression in poverty. When he was in grade 9, a teacher took pity on him and bought him some shoes. Things got so tough for him that he had to quit school at age 15 and get a job at Borden's Dairy Products to support himself and his struggling family. However, he persevered and got certification in the new trade of electrician and eventually took enough night school courses to be accepted to university. So, he decided he would leave his job as electrician at Shell Oil in Chemical Valley of Sarnia to begin university studies and our family would move to the farm. During our year on the farm, dad commuted by car to London daily with Ms. Ritchie, a young university student studying languages. He helped out every night with the evening milking chores. I have a strong memory of him sitting on a lawn chair near the woods the following Spring reading through his notes to prepare for upcoming final exams.

With my parents, Jack and Noreen circa 1961

Noreen

My mother, Noreen, probably had some mixed feelings about all this. Just when our family was becoming comfortably settled for 13 years in Sarnia, it seemed like quite a risk for dad to quit his career as an electrician and begin a career as a minister with her probably supporting him through his university years until he was ordained. Years later, she expressed these very doubts about this move to me. On the other hand, her mother obviously needed some help and companionship on the farm. Mom took on a part-time job as a registered nurse at Alexandra Hospital, often doing shift work like 3:00 - 11:00 p.m. or the midnight shift. Therefore, she had a lot of duties to perform. She made the lunches for us kids to take to school and busied herself with the daily domestic cooking and house cleaning chores. I have no memory of her ever being in the barn doing milking chores or helping in grandma's vegetable garden.

Phil

I'm not sure what my brother thought of the move to the farm. He had many friends his age in Sarnia that he would have to say goodbye to. However, he and grandma had a special bond and he became very helpful in the daily operations of the farm doing both morning and evening milking chores while going to grade eight. A neighbour down the road, Mr. Atterbury, would take him out hunting for groundhogs. It was on the farm where I first saw a box full of bullets. Phil showed me how to load and fire the rifle as I experienced it's "kick" into my shoulder when it went off. However, I wasn't much interested in guns and was too young to be trusted with them on my own anyway.

Brenda

My sister, Brenda, just turned seven in the summer we moved to the farm. We had left a suburban street in Sarnia that was teeming with young baby boomers to come to the farm where the nearest neighbour's kids were very far away. I recently asked my sister what she remembered about the farm and she replied, "I found it being everyone for themselves". She makes a very good point. With grandma and Phil completing morning milking chores, dad on the way to London for school and mom doing shift work, Brenda and I often had to find our own breakfast then get ourselves ready for school. I recall playing Monopoly and Chinese Checkers with my sister and playing in the hay mow, but I can now see how she was then in a position to grow up independently very fast at age 7.

Phoebe and George

George Powell and Aunt Phoebe lived right across the road. Phoebe was grandma's younger sister. Phoebe had poor eyesight, was nearly deaf and she spoke with a nasal sound that made her difficult to understand. I once asked grandma what happed to Phoebe and she said she got sick with scarlet fever when she was young. A terrible disease from the recent past that can destroy lives, but is now entirely treatable with antibiotic medications. I was in their small house once and there was a large quilting loom set up. Since Phoebe was never in the barn and rarely ever in the main farm house, she spent her days cooking meals for her husband George and working on quilting.

George Powell was a very old man in the last year of his life and someone that the word "trudge" was meant for. Plodding head down to the barn in dark blue overalls, his mood was always set at miserable and depressed. I sometimes found myself wanting to talk to him, but I was constantly dismissed like a pesky fly as he trudged past. In trying to determine why George was so unhappy, mom once pointed out a small collapsing farm near the tracks and Ingersoll Golf Course and said it used to belong to George. Perhaps it was swallowed up by the 1956 construction of Highway 401 and he received very little compensation for a lifetime of effort at farming. Whatever the cause, he was probably the most miserable person I have ever met.

Grandma's sister Phoebe with husband George Powell

Baptist Church in Salford, now a "Dutch Reformed" church

Arriving

I have a rather clear recollection of moving from Sarnia to the farm in the summer of 1966. Currie and Dorothy Way and their six children had come to Sarnia for a late June weekend visit. They had both been classmates of my mom and Dorothy (Bowman) was her best friend in childhood. Noreen's journal affectionately refers to Dorothy as "Dot". It was decided after supper that I would ride back to the farm with the Way family. I was curled up in the back end of their station wagon with brothers Gene and George and we played a game of counting all the Volkswagon Beetles along the highway. I was dropped off at grandma's farm and went in to greet her by myself. It was possibly one of the only times I was at the farm with grandma without the rest of my family. I recall as dusk approached skipping and singing with joy down the laneway as school was just out and a new life was about to begin here on the farm.

The next day was a Sunday, and I went to the Baptist Church in Salford with grandma and I'm pretty sure Claude Banbury was one of the men who collected the money at offertory. During the church service they served communion with tiny little glasses of grape juice. I recall thinking that Baptists are rather skimpy since that little bit of juice wasn't enough quench my thirst, and grandma wasn't even sure I was supposed to have any because I wasn't confirmed yet.

Later that evening, grandma had some kind of church meeting to attend to, so I was sent over to aunt Gladys' house. I recall sitting and watching an episode of "Bonanza" on their TV as it was one of my favourite television shows at the time. A few days later it was July 1st and I recall being with Keith Wilson's kids (Dennis and David) in grandma's dining room watching tv. I knew enough about Canadian history at age 9 to tell the young boys that July 1st was Canada's Birthday and that the nation was 99 years old.

Maggie

The rest of my family arrived the next day and a decision had to be made about getting a new dog. Keith Wilson's hired man, Jim Barker, had a dog that had given birth to a whole litter of mixed mutts and word went out asking if grandma wanted any of the puppies. It was decided that we could take one of the puppies and so we adopted a brown dog we came to call "Maggie". This young dog was cute and cuddly and a perfect companion for a nine year-old. However, grandma already had a beautiful older collie dog, Cindy. I recall Cindy snapping and growling at Maggie whenever I lavished too much attention on the puppy. Life for Maggie was also rather challenging in the barn. We didn't buy dog food - just a bowl of cow's milk set out at feeding time. As soon as the bowl was filled, a swarm of about 13 barn cats would slink towards the bowl and push Maggie away. We once took a picture of Maggie looking forlorn at the milk bowl surrounded by feral cats.

Milking

It was during this summer that the rhythm of barn chores commenced for the family. Milking chores were primarily performed by grandma, George and brother Phil assisted frequently by father, Jack. The 40 black-and-white Holstein cows were milked twice a day, first at sunrise (6:00 a.m.), then at dusk (6:00 p.m.). At the time, an electric suction portable milking machine was attached to the udders of each cow and it took about five minutes for each cow to complete the milking. The warm milk that was drawn from the cow was then taken to the "milking parlour" and poured into a large cooling tank. I was given three chores; First I would fetch eight bales of hay from the hay mow and open them up to feed the cows. Then I would fill a cup with blue disinfectant and apply it to each cow's teet that had finished milking. My other main chore was to feed very young calves. This was done by mixing a few cups of pancake batter-like powder called Sur-Gain with water into a pail, then cup my hand into the mix and coax the calf into sucking my hand to get nourishment. I guess my nine-year-old hand was just the right size to trick a calf into thinking it was sucking on a real cow! There was one cute baby calf I came to call "Buster", but grandma frowned on me treating the calf too much like a pet. I came to see what she meant when Buster ended up on our dinner table and I refused to eat.

Getting the cows into the barn and ready for milking was something quite graceful and rather astounding to behold. All barn doors would open up at once and every cow would line up at their allocated door and start walking into the barn. Silage would be placed in each manger. It looked like chaos with all cows plodding everywhere through the barn. However, every cow knew by habit exactly which stanchion to put their head into and all cows were packed in exact order ready for milking in about 2 minutes. When I walked behind the row of cows I had to keep alert for the possibility that at any time a cow could squat and release a splatter of urine or manure into the gutter and splash onto my clothes. As soon as I saw a cow begin to squat, I quickly turned away.

<u>Animal Farm</u>

There were a variety of farm animals. Cindy the collie dog slept under the back porch and guarded the laneway. There were at least 13 unnamed barn cats led by a large Persian matriarch that none of the other cats messed with. Most of the cats were feral and interbred subsisting on field mice. It was the last year we kept pigs. There were 2 sows and two boars and a scattering of piglets. Aside from the 40 milking cows, we kept about six young heifer cows in a pen within the barn. Aside from "Kicky" the cow, none of the cows were given names except "Blackie". She was the only cow with a completely black head. She was also the only cow you could "ride"! I recall grandma perching my sister, Brenda, on top of the cow. I also recall sitting on top of this cow right there in the barn with all the other cows. Blackie just stood there motionless. I never thought to ask just how they knew this particular cow was tame enough to let little children ride on top - but it was sure a fun experience! In the late spring when I was assigned the task of fetching the cows from pasture, I recall searching out Blackie the cow to lead the herd to the barn. She just seemed to be the most intelligent, friendly and co-operative of the entire herd.

Along with the herd of cows and a few pigs, we also had two beautiful draft horses; Goldie and Queenie. Goldie had a golden mane and Queenie had a black mane. They were always paired together in their own pasture near the barn away from the cows. I recall Jim Barker riding each horse completely "bareback" without harnesses. I think Queenie was the younger one because he could really get her to gallop fast. Once there was a late night thunderstorm and the horses were in the pasture next to the house. Flash lightning would briefly illuminate the horses, then the thunder would spook them to another part of the pasture. Suddenly another flash of lightning would illuminate them in a completely different position. It was just one of those dramatic events where the mix of horses in a violent rainstorm conjures unforgettable memories.

Once in the dead of winter, I remember checking out the horse stall attached to the implement building where the farm machinery was kept. I slipped past their large hind legs and climbed up into the small hay mow above their heads. I remember looking down on the horses and thinking what a boring life they lead. Tied up all day in the horse barn and let out only once in the morning if the ice wasn't too bad. They just stood there, dad after day, calmly chewing on their oats.

There were three main crops grown on the farm; hay, wheat and corn. These crops were rotated so that if wheat was grown one year, the next year it would be planted with corn, followed by hay. After three rotations, the field was left fallow for a year to facilitate soil recovery and used as a meadow to put the cows out to pasture. Everything that our livestock ate was grown in the fields around the farm.

Feasting

Bringing in the summertime harvest required a lot of extra manpower. Someone was needed to drive the tractor and combine, then another person to pile the hay bales onto the wagon. Next, the bales were loaded onto an elevator to be taken to the top of the barn. Then you needed a couple of people in the hay mow to sort and stack the bales right up to the rafters. Grandma usually hired three or four extra labourers to accomplish these tasks. To make it more appealing for the extra workers, she would host a noontime feast. Roast beef and gravy, mashed potatoes, carrots, corn-on-the cob, then apple pie rounded out the daily banquet. It was not uncommon for ten to twelve people seated round the kitchen table enjoying a wholesome dinner as a wonderful break from tedious chores.

A picture emerges of just how hard grandma worked every day when she was well into her 60's. Up at 6:00 a.m. to start the morning milking, she would return from the barn around 9:00 a.m. to begin preparing the daily feast. This required peeling by hand about 15 potatoes and other preparations to have the extensive meal ready by noon. After lunch, the clean up chores in the kitchen took at least a couple of hours. Then she might take a quick trip into town to pick up more provisions for the next day. It was then time to get set up and engage in the evening milking chores. The evening meal was usually leftovers from the afternoon feast, but another round of kitchen cleanup took her to about 8:00 o'clock. I remember getting ready to go to bed around 9:00 o'clock and seeing her from the bedroom window still in her vegetable garden pulling out potatoes and carrots and doing the necessary weeding. The woman would work non-stop every day for about 16 hours throughout the summer.

Sayings

Grandma had a few wise sayings that she passed on to me. One is "If you can't say anything *good* about someone...don't say anything." Over the years I have tried to heed my grandmother's advice because there are many situations where keeping quiet about someone's faults is much better than broadcasting your opinion. Often your unkind words will come back to haunt you. Another homespun proverb was "If you burn your ass...you have to sit on the blisters". She rarely spoke in profanities, but coming from her it has special poignancy. People will suffer the consequences of their actions. I think she was talking about a relative, but since I choose to adhere to her first advice about not saying anything bad about people, I'll decline to offer my opinion on who I think she was talking about.

Melancholy

Nobody tells you anything when you're nine years old! Henry, the hired man, was digging a large hole in the corner of the cornfield at the back of the barn and I wanted to know why. He just said, "It's for Cindy".

I didn't know what to think. I was horrified. It couldn't be true!

There is nothing quite so majestic as a beautiful collie dog. With an aquiline nose, athletic thin body and long hair swaying in the breeze with each step, a collie is one of the most gorgeous breeds of dog in the world, although Welsh Corgis probably have more "personality".

Cindy lived under our front porch nestled in bales of fresh straw. She would occasionally be seen in the barn yard but I have no recollection of her being in the barn. Despite all the mud and manure mess of the farm, she kept herself very clean. She was friendly and engaging and always up for a game of retrieving ball.

Her domain was the back yard of the farm house and she was very protective of our family. If anyone came down the farm lane or drove in, she would bark a serious warning to let us know we had a visitor. When visitors arrived, she would sniff them out and generally let them pass if they were known to her.

Back in the early 1960's there was a TV show called "Lassie". I can still remember the mournful whistle theme and Lassie pawing at the screen at the conclusion of each episode. I fancied myself as Timmy, the farm boy who had weekly adventures with Lassie. Since I was now living on the farm, Cindy was a great companion to have.

Despite her adventurous spirit and wonderful disposition, Cindy had a fatal flaw; She would run after cars or anything that moved fast.

The fastest truck I ever remember coming down the farm lane was the heavy milk truck that did its daily run at about noon. He would roar down the lane towards the barn and Cindy would go chasing after the truck in hot pursuit. As the truck kicked up a cloud of dust, Cindy would bark incessantly running alongside the vehicle and occasionally sniping at the large wheels.

Eventually this behaviour caught up with Cindy. I wasn't there to see it, but one day in the early summer of 1966 I noticed she spent the entire day sitting under the porch hardly moving. A couple of days later I saw her limping slowly from the house to the barn. She must have got caught on the truck's tire as it rolled over her long legs.

Cindy was never the same after that. She was unable to clean herself and after a time I noticed dust and dirt caking her long hair. She didn't interact with anyone and pretty much kept to herself under the porch. It was also the time when we were playing and fawning over the new puppy, Maggie and often ignoring Cindy.

I'm not sure how or when grandma decided to ask the vet to put her down, but later in the summer the veterinarian was asked to give Cindy a lethal injection to put her out of her misery. I still remember the date, August 17, 1966.

On the day she was put down, I don't remember anyone else there except Henry, the vet and I. "You can't just kill her, it's Cindy!"..."I know she's been hit by the truck, but she still gets around, OK".

Henry tried to console me saying that Cindy was in terrible pain, hardly ate and couldn't keep herself clean. It was what had to be done.

The hired hand dug a fairly large hole in the field behind the barn, then together we fetched Cindy from under the porch. Despite her limping pain, Cindy did her slow death march to her grave.

We laid her down beside the hole. The end was very near. Cindy was such a brave beautiful dog even in death. I remember petting her head and seeing the vet pull a needle out of his black bag. He said, "this won't hurt"...and "this won't take long".

Cindy looked up at me one last time as he gave her the injection. Within seconds she drifted into an endless sleep.

There were no prayers or any other ceremony for Cindy that day. There is no marker for her grave. I fought back my tears and gave her one last loving stroke on her head. Together we pulled her into the grave and slowly covered her. All that was left was the memory of a beautiful, intelligent collie dog that was once a part of our family...then was no more.

Cindy the Collie dog

Day Tripper

Dairy farmers are tied to the land with chores that make it extremely difficult to take even one day of vacation. The cows have to be milked twice a day and if you want to go somewhere, you have to train and pay someone to take over your chores in your absence.

Just before school started in September, our family decided to take a day trip with grandma to Niagara Falls, located about a 3-hour drive from the farm. This required starting chores a half-hour early - then quickly wolfing down breakfast and washing up to get on our way by 9:00 o'clock. We made it to Niagara Falls before noon, bought a quick lunch, then saw the brand new Skylon Tower and took in one of the museums on Clifton Hill. After a hasty stroll in front of the falls, it was time to pile into the car and head back to the farm. So after only three hours at Niagara Falls, we drive home to fetch the cows out of the pasture to commence the evening milking chores. That three hours in Niagara Falls was the only "vacation" that grandma had the entire summer. There is no such thing as a "day off" for families involved in dairy farming.

Schooling

Schooling in the small village of Salford proved to be an interesting challenge for me. I had completed grade three in a 12-room Sarnia suburb at Woodland elementary school. The school was a sea of white faces where the only visible minorities in a population of 400 children were Dr. Wong's kids. I recall the entire school population forming a circle around the flag pole on a cold February morning while the principal hoisted the brand new Canadian maple leaf flag for the first time in February, 1965. It was a time when students who excelled were promoted by "skipping" a grade. I was one of five students in my class of 30 chosen to "accelerate" through grade 3, then complete grade 4 and 5 together the next year. It was intended as a gradual process by completing three grades in two years.

However, my arrival at Salford elementary school presented a dilemma. Oxford County didn't have a program of accelerating or skipping grades. Children stayed in their age-appropriate class. Would I go to grade four, even though I had successfully completed an advanced grade three curriculum? It would seem like a setback. On the other hand, vaulting to grade five without completing most of grade four was going to be an obvious risk to my education. Furthermore, the grade four class was conducted in a one-room school where Salford Road meets the Culloden Road. It would mean my brother and sister would be going to Salford and I would be going to the smaller school out in the countryside. After some deliberation, it was decided that I would be placed in grade five, my progress would be monitored and I would be sent to grade four if my grades were suffering. I took this opportunity seriously and recall studying for tests and trying my best at school. Thankfully, everything worked out and I remained in grade five.

Compounding the challenging experience of schooling was the split grade 5/6 class I found myself in at Salford. I was the youngest person in the class on one side of the room and students two years older were instructed on the other side of the room. There were a few hefty athletic grade six farm boys in my class like Paul Bartram, Ross Wilson and Donny Pearson. There were also a few 12-year-old girls who seemed well past puberty As a teacher, it is well known that educators "teach to the middle" of split classes with slightly higher expectations of grade five students and many "shared" experiences with the grade six students.

One important component of the grade four curriculum is teaching kids the transition from printing to writing. I recall early in September watching the kids around me using cursive writing while I tried to loop my scrawled printing to look like writing. I quickly gave myself a crash course in writing and accomplished in two weeks what I should have been taught for most of grade four. To this day, my handwriting is rather strange and I still don't know what the capital letter Q is in writing. I recently read a newspaper article stating that cursive writing will no longer be taught at school as the instructional time is needed to hone computer keypad skills. All I can say is that it's about time! My dad inadvertently helped me out in this endeavour to learn cursive writing by having me write out 50 times; "I will not toss firecrackers in the wood stove" and "I will not disrupt my sister's music lesson."

Riding the school bus was a new experience for me and my siblings. We had to be ready for school by 8:30 a.m. and stood in the unheated breezeway room facing East. As soon as we saw the bus come over the hill a kilometre away, we walked to the end of the lane to be picked up. The bus driver was a crusty non-nonsense man known as Mr. Nancekivelle and the bus drove out to Culloden Road, then South to the next concession before turning East on Salford Road towards the village, picking up kids all along the way. We arrived at the school about five minutes before it started.

Salford Public School

Music Lessons

In September, my sister and I also started music lessons with Mrs. Ranney in Salford. Grandma had a nice upright grand piano in the parlour where I practiced my scales and arpeggios for the Saturday morning lessons. I found myself drawn to the piano and willingly went to practice for about half an hour after supper. I don't remember anyone hounding me to rehearse my piano lessons - I just enjoyed working on the songs until they sounded good. Mrs. Ranney was an excellent, motivating teacher who guided me through music piano instruction for the next eight years. Perhaps it was the isolation of the farm and the lack of technological or social distractions, but going to the piano and trying to make the songs sound good was a very enjoyable experience for me. Since I eventually went on to the Faculty of Music at the University of Western Ontario and receive a Bachelor of Music and become a high school music teacher in Kitchener, I can credit that piano in the farmhouse parlour as the instrument that determined my destiny.

Technology

Today, we have landlines and cell phones, digital flat screen televisions with optic cable and remotes, computers with wifi internet connections and a variety of gaming systems. Technology was not like that on the farm in the 1960's. Television and telephones were rather primitive compared to today. One could receive two channels on the black and white television; channel 10 was CFPL in London and channel 13 was CKCO in Kitchener. One didn't really need a remote channel changer because you only needed to get up and change the channel once to observe the totality of programming. On Friday night you had the choice between "Don Messer's Jubilee" or "Polka Time". I often found myself turning off the tv and going to play the piano. On the other hand, I recall watching some wonderful movies like "Shane" and "Black Beauty" by myself on rainy Saturday afternoons.

Grandma only watched one television show for one hour once a week. That show was Red Skelton's Comedy Hour on Tuesday nights. After coming in from doing the evening chores and before going to bed, she found herself giggling and laughing at the hilarious antics of Klem Kadiddlehopper, George Appleby and Freddie the Freeloader - all clowning characters portrayed by Red Skelton. I often found myself watching this show with her because I also enjoyed the clowning humour. However, aside from the occasional hockey game, that once-a-week viewing was about all the television that grandma watched. Even at that, she probably felt guilty for allowing this small diversion when there was so much work to be done on the farm.

The black rotary dial telephone was located in the hallway beside the stairs. The operating system in those days was known as a "party line". This meant that our phone line was shared with other families down the concession. We had a specific ring code of "long-short-short" for identification and were not supposed to pick up the phone if it was any other combination of rings. You would pick up the telephone and hear perhaps Louise Wilson, Marlene Barker or Mrs. Atterbury on the phone. I recall grandma picking up the phone once and saying, "Oh, hi Louise, I just wanted to use the phone to find out about the cattle auction in Norwich." The trick to listening in on other conversations was to pick up the phone at the exact time the intended recipient picked up the receiver and stay really quiet. I must admit that as an occasionally bored 9 year-old, I engaged in this type of surreptitious espionage. At the present time, there is a nationwide discussion about privacy rights and the government's secret eavesdropping on citizen's internet data and phone conversations. I wonder how many of these politicians lived through the era of the "party line".

Pork

A remarkable event that took place in the fall of 1966 was the birth of pigs in the barn. Grandma somehow knew that the large pregnant sow was ready to give birth and strung a row of red heating lights in the stall to warm up the newly arriving piglets. Then she and Phil waited well past midnight to assist in the birthing process and ensure none of the babies died of exposure or got crushed by the mother pig. All through the night, little baby pigs popped out of the sow at ten minute intervals. Working together, grandma and Phil cleaned and warmed each newborn, then carefully set each baby to suckle the mother. It is quite a sight to see 15 little baby piglets squirming wildly in a row beside the sow seeking nourishment and survival. Grandma and Phil stayed up all night to assist in the birth, then did the morning milking chores and got on with the next day without any rest at all.

<u>Church</u>

Sunday mornings meant hurrying up chores, washing up, putting on your best clothes and going to church. While grandma went off to the Salford Baptist church, our family drove into town and attended St. James Anglican church since dad was studying to be an Anglican minister. I recall the beautiful autumn colours of the trees along Canterbury Street in Ingersoll as we made our way to church. The majestic red carpeted interior was magnificent to behold and much more lavish than the rural or suburban church interiors I was used to. Our family took up a pew about half way down on the left right behind Dr. Westman's family. The Anglican rituals of white robed processions, chanting in Latin and kneeling on prayer benches was something I was used to in Sarnia, but everything here just seemed much more solemn and formal. Thus began a close association with St. James Anglican church that continued for the next 15 years as I later took on various church responsibilities as altar boy and assistant organist.

Another activity at the church that I participated in was Cub Scouts. The club met every Tuesday evening in the basement of St. James and I usually went there with Stephen Sadler with his dad, Ray, usually driving. It was here that I memorized the scout creed; "I promise to do my best, to do my duty to God and the Queen and to keep the law of the Wolf Cub Pack and to do a good turn for someone every day." Pretty good values to live up to.

St. James Anglican Church Interior

<u>Woodshed</u>

As winter approached, it was time to stock the woodshed. Grandma hired three men who went into the woods and brought back large branches of dead or dying trees on a flatbed wagon. Right beside the farmhouse next to the woodshed they set up a large circular saw powered by a tractor. All day long we heard the buzzing blades as they cut the branches down to usable size and stacked the wood in the small room beside the kitchen. This provided the fuel for the large woodstove that heated the house and cooked our meals for the next year.

In the age before plastic, we created very little garbage on the farm. There was no rural garbage truck that came by to cart off bags of garbage like today. If it could be burned - it went into the wood stove. If it was organic, such as food waste and potato peels, it went into the "slop pail". This was the stuff that was fed to the pigs. There was no such thing as plastic containers as many grocery items from milk and pop to mustard were in a glass jar. Today there is an effort to reduce garbage, but 50 years ago everything was used up and very little garbage was created.

<u>Christmas</u>

Christmas was a magical time for a kid on the farmhouse. The parlour was decked out in red and green and a real Spruce tree was brought in from the woods. Brenda recalls the anticipation of getting up early on Christmas morning and sneaking down to the parlour before anyone else was awake. One present I recall getting was a 5 dollar bill from Claude Banbury that was wrapped in a small box inside 7 increasingly larger boxes. It took about 10 minutes to unwrap it - but it was lots of fun. The afternoon feast of turkey with all the trimmings included many of grandma's relatives seated round the large dining room table. There weren't enough chairs to seat everyone so we decided to use the piano bench for two people to sit on. The evening milking chores went slower than usual as everyone was a bit sleepy from eating all that turkey.

New Years Eve was no big deal at all on the farm. I don't recall anyone staying up to ring in the new year. Everyone just went to bed at the usual 10:00 p.m. from the usual exhaustion of daily chores with another day of hard work awaiting. The new year that was dawning was a special year for Canada - Centennial Year! Our nation was turning 100 years old in 1967.

Phil, Brian and Brenda on Christmas morning

Spirits

One interesting thing about living on the farm at this time was the complete absence of alcohol. Grandma certainly didn't drink as her Baptist faith forbade it, and mom and dad never purchased any alcohol as budgets were very tight with dad taking the year off work to attend university. At school, the local United Church minister, Reverend Menses would come to speak to our class once a week and rail against the evils of alcohol. It was a time when memories of the great Prohibition experiment of the 1920's still lingered in the hearts of rural farmers and complete abstinence was the attitude of most of grandma's friends and relatives.

The winter of 1967 was a relatively mild one, however the previous winter was particularly harsh with large drifts of snow piling up everywhere. A temporary wood fence was strung up from the back porch to the unused chicken coop and the snow mound created from drifting snow was probably twelve feet high. We built an amazing ice fortress of snow with many connecting tunnels into the large drift and played there for hours one afternoon.

Birthday

My birthday arrived on February 17th and I turned ten years old. My family had a surprise for me. They had secretly contacted some of my school friends such as Bobby Belore and the Wagner boys and they began arriving in the early afternoon. We all went tobogganing on the hill past the back field then came back to the house to warm our feet by the wood stove. We feasted on hot dogs and I blew out the ten candles on the birthday cake. It was great to have a bunch of classmates over. Interestingly, it was the only time I recall having friends my age over to the farm.

Snowball

The last dumping of snow came in early March. I was out on the schoolyard at afternoon recess playing with my grade five friends. Suddenly a snowball smacked right into my right eye socket. The pain was really intense as I cried and sobbed for the next hour. I was taken into principal Mrs. Gould's office where she wrapped a bandage across my head. She called grandma who came and picked me up and took me back to the farm. Later that day, dad drove me to see Dr. John Lawson. He examined my eye and concluded that although the lens had been scratched, it would eventually heal with no permanent damage. Whew! For the next week, I wore an eye patch with cotton stuffed into my eye socket. I probably looked like a very sad pirate. The culprit who threw the snowball was Brock Barrett who phoned me at night to tell me he was sorry. It's probably a good reason why throwing snowballs on schoolyards is prohibited.

Shooting

As winter slowly disappeared, I had a disturbing encounter with death on the farm. There was this really old cow with a sagging back and withered udder that had dried up and was no longer capable of giving milk. I recall grandma and George whispering about the circumstances as they stopped milking her for a few days. The next Saturday morning a large truck pulled into the farmyard. George led the old cow out of the barn directly behind the truck. The driver attached a cable to the cow's legs. Then he pulled out a large rifle and placed it right between the eyes of the cow. Bam! The rifle went off and the cow's legs stiffened, then fell to the ground. Instant death. The cow was then dragged up into the back of the truck. The driver detached the cable from the cow, closed the back hatch and drove off. So this is what happens to cows that are too old to give milk. A rather brutal death.

Cats

Around the same time, something had to be done about the barn cats. A hideous disease had spread through all the cats. The disease was called distemper. A thick mucus crust formed over their eyes that practically sealed them shut. They slowly crawled when we approached instead of the usual scamper. They constantly meow-moaned with a faint whispering cry. Fewer and fewer cats made it to the daily milk bowl. Having seen enough wretchedness from the suffering animals, Phil and I took the remaining ones near death and shot them behind the silo. The sickness killed all the cats.

Tractor Driving

One important job that is necessary on the farm is clearing large stones from the fields that have been heaved up during the Spring thaw. Keith and Jim wanted to clear the stones from the field across from mom's birthplace, next to highway 401. Since two men gathering stones and placing them on a flatbed wagon would make the work go twice as fast, it was decided that I would accompany them and get a quick lesson on how to drive a tractor. The idea was for me to drive slowly around the perimeter of the field while they brought the large rocks to the wagon. However, keeping the left foot alternating between the clutch and brake while gradually engaging the gears and simultaneously accelerating with the right foot and steering were concepts that required more time than the 5-minute hothouse lesson I received on how to drive a tractor. They eventually put the tractor into first gear and had me drive very slowly a few times around the field, but I could tell they were somewhat disappointed in my driving abilities. However, this quick lesson in stick-shift driving came in handy when I got summer jobs as a mini bus driver and lawn cutter for the Ingersoll Parks and Recreation Department ten years later.

Leaf Nation

Back in 1966-67 there were only six professional hockey teams; the Original Six. There were only two rounds of playoffs with the Stanley Cup Finals decided before the end of April. Like a lot of people, our interest in watching tv hockey peaked at playoff time. That spring brought a classic national battle between Canada's two teams; the Montreal Canadiens and the Toronto Maple Leafs. Even now, I can name many players right off the top of my head; Dave Keon,... Pete Mahovolich,... Tim Horton...and goalie Terry Sawchuck with coach "Punch" Imlach. On the opposing side was the only person I ever heard of with the name "Gump" before the movie "Forest Gump". Montreal's goalie was "Gump" Worsley. Their fine team was led by Jean Beliveau and coached by "Toe" Blake. Wonderful Sporty names. By 1967 it was rather common for Toronto to win the playoffs since they had won three Stanley Cups earlier in the decade. If I had only known that this Stanley Cup was the last they would win in my lifetime, I would probably have cheered them on harder than I did.

As a kid, this sporting event made for exciting television viewing. However, as a ten-year old child, the advertisements from major sponsor ESSO left a lasting impression. Animated graphics of a playful tiger cavorting across the tv screen and a catchy jingle "Hold That Tiger" were very successful marketing tricks from that era. I recall wanting dad to get his gas at an ESSO station because they gave out little stuffed tiger tails with each fill-up.

<u>Death of George</u>

As the daylight stretched longer and the newly planted crops began to sprout all over the countryside, George Powel's health took a dramatic turn for the worse. He had a horrible racking cough and seemed more miserable than ever as he continued to trudge along the laneway for morning and evening milking chores. Suddenly on May 26, 1966 I heard that George had died in hospital. I didn't even know that George had gone to hospital the day before. I always kept clear of him.

<u>Clayton Cuthbert</u>

With George Powell gone and the busy harvesting season approaching, it was necessary to find a hired hand to replace him. That person was Clayton Cuthbert. I didn't know it at the time, but he was uncle Clarence Cuthbert's brother; my grandmother's first husband's sister's husband's brother! He had a sunny, cheerful disposition and would actually stop and talk to me - something George never did. Clayton was also very good with horses. He harnessed Goldie and Queenie and brought them to the back field and hitched them to the large rake. I have a fond memory of him driving the horses through the field of fresh cut hay smiling and waving at me. He obviously enjoyed working with horses and doing chores the old-fashioned way. This was one of the few times I saw the horses working and probably the last time they were ever used on the farm. That sight of them in June 1967 pulling the rake through the field was the very end of a century long tradition of real horsepower.

Bobby Belore

During my school year at Salford, I made one really good friend; Bobby Belore. He was tall, lanky and rather quiet as we would find ourselves eating lunch and playing together at recess. He lived about five km. East of Salford. One Saturday in late spring I rode my bicycle all the way to his house and thought it such an accomplishment. His family had a really interesting vocation; they raised and trained racehorses! Their horses were the sleek standard-bred type, nothing like our large workhorses. These were trained to trot at a fast pace and pull a cart and driver. One Saturday night, I was invited by Bobby to go to London Raceway to watch his dad race a few of their horses. I recall cheering him on as he came in first place in one very tight race. Bobby and I were invited down to the track to join his family for a congratulatory photo. What a neat thing for a kid like me to be associated with a winner and pose for a picture in front of a few thousand people!

Singing

It is important to remember that 1967 was Centennial Year, the celebration of 100 years of Canada as a nation. All across Canada were special projects as the festive mood permeated the national consciousness. In particular, what I remember most about that year were two songs taught to us at school; *Ca-na-da*, and *Give Us A Place to Stand*. We had a particularly motivating itinerant music teacher named Mr. Smith that came to our class and taught us those songs. He also taught these same songs to the grade7 / 8 class next door with all the harmonies and counter-melodies included. As a culminating activity, the large sliding wall separating our two classrooms was opened up and everyone from grade 5 to grade 8 performed the music for ourselves. It was just one of those memorable musical experiences that has remained with me and probably stimulated me to pursue music as a career.

Simcoe

Another project that our class undertook was the day-long school trip. As a split grade 5 / 6 class, we knew we couldn't travel as far as Toronto or Niagara Falls, because these trips were the special destinations of grades seven and eight. Our class had an open discussion about where we might go since London, Brantford and Simcoe were strong contenders. It was finally decided that our class would spend the day in Simcoe. Our teacher, Mrs. Richardson, had the class draft letters to the Simcoe Chamber of Commerce and determine what tourism opportunities beckoned. Our class had little bake sales and fundraisers to defray the cost of the bus. Towards the end of June, we spent a very enjoyable day touring the beautiful park, jam factory and ice cream factory in Simcoe, ending the afternoon at the municipal swimming pool.

A few weeks before the school trip I received secret notes from two different girls asking if I would sit with them on the bus to Simcoe. One was from Barb Sivyer, someone who also shared a passion for music, and Betty Anne Lonsberry, a nice girl with reddish-brown hair. Unfortunately for them, I had my eye on the pretty blond Dutch girl who arrived in the middle of the year and never said a word in class. To solve this tangled childhood love quadrangle, I solved the issue of who I would join with on the bus by sitting with my good friend Bobby Belore.

Baseball

A major recreational activity promoted by the school at the end of the year was baseball. Since there was no gymnasium, baseball seemed to be the only recreational activity undertaken by my class because this game can include everyone. It was also co-ed underhand pitched softball, where all the boys and girls of our class formed a team. I soon came to realize that I was not the absolute worst player in the line-up since some of the girls ran from the ball if it was batted to them. Our team travelled to three other schools for friendly competition against their grade 5 / 6 classes; Verchoyle, Brownsville and Ostrander. It was great fun touring the other small country village schools.

Herding

After George Powell died, I was given a very important chore. I stayed on the bus a little longer after Phil and Brenda departed and got off where Dennis Wilson reached his destination. Next to their farm was a field where all of grandma's cows were put to pasture. It was my job to round them all up and walk them down the gravel road to our farm to prepare them for milking. Concerned that the herd might go the wrong way and walk out onto the highway, grandma assured me that the cows would know what to do. Just be sure to walk them and don't make them run. She was right! When I arrived at the pasture, I would seek out Blackie the cow as all the Holstein bovines slowly stood up then walked toward the gate. Blackie led the entire herd of 40 cows out of the gate and down the road to the farm. I just had to walk behind them and make sure the gate to our farm was open. In retrospect, it was quite a responsibility to trust the entire herd of cows to a 10-year-old kid, but I was successful in getting all the cows out of the pasture and down the concession all by myself.

KFC

School was out and the big day arrived! It was July 1st, 1967 and the nation was celebrating its 100th birthday. What I remember most about that day was going with my family to Brantford for a parade. I was with my good friend Bobby Belore. At the front of the parade was an old white haired man with a tight goatee, string tie and trademark white jacket. It was Colonel Sanders, the founder of Kentucky Fried Chicken! It seems odd now that an iconic American entrepreneur would lead a Canadian parade on a day of national celebration, but I've come to realize that most parades are just opportunities for businesses to advertise their products.

Expo

A week later, our family traveled to Montreal to see Expo 67. This was a very successful international exposition and showcased the latest innovations from many countries around the world. I recall riding the monorail through the giant geodesic dome and taking in all the presentations from many pavilions and thinking that this is what the future would look like.

Expo 67 site in Montreal. Photo by Jack Smith

Leaving

Soon after we returned from our vacation, it was time to pack up and leave the farm for good and move to Ingersoll. Dad got a job as an electrician at Essex Wire where he would help make electrical components for cars. Mom continued as a full time nurse at Alexandra Hospital. Phil would enrol in grade 9 at Ingersoll District Collegiate Institute. Brenda would join me at Victory Memorial School (VMS). We found a place on Oxford Street, just five houses away from St. James Anglican church and right across the road from VMS. The house was a duplex where the landlord Danny Dunlop's family lived on one side, and our family lived on the other side. Interestingly, the neighbour next to our house was Mr. Riddolls, the high school music teacher. He would become a very important role model for my life and inspire me to take up a career as an educator.

We moved to this house in August 1967. We lived on the left side, Dunlops
on the right. Mr. Riddolls lived next door on the right.

Last Day

My memory of grandma's last day on the homestead came when I walked the tracks from our new house in Ingersoll back to the farm. I recall her pegging some sheets onto the long clothesline that stretched from the back porch. She helped me get the lawnmower started and I spent the next two hours cutting the lawn. After a refreshing cold drink in the kitchen, I stepped out of the farmhouse for the last time and walked the tracks back to my new home. For me, the brief time of living on the farm had passed. She had sold the farm to Rick Wilson and his wife Susanne. It was certainly time for a new younger generation to manage the farm. For grandma, a lifetime of toil working and managing a dairy farm was coming to an end.

There was a small plaque that hung in the farmhouse kitchen across from the wood stove. It read, **"The hurrier I go, the behinder I get**." Sort of a homage to the methodical tortoise way of approaching life as opposed to the frantic hare. It seemed to sum up the manner in which grandma approached all her tasks with poise, dignity and grace. I don't know if she packed it to put in her new house or left these nuggets of wisdom for the new family to enjoy.

The farm in 2013

Retirement

Grandma retired to a comfortable house on Holcroft Street across from the golf course. She purchased a pool table and a color television and made it a wonderful refuge for the grandkids to visit. For the next three years of her life, she took up curling in winter and golf in the summer. I wonder what she thought of these recreational diversions after a lifetime of more purposeful exertion on the farm.

She drew her last breath on Thursday February 4th, 1970. It was a sudden and completely unexpected death. Mom said she died in her sleep of heart failure. As she lay dying, I wonder if she had time to reflect upon her life. Her childhood growing up with five sisters and a brother on a farm outside Ingersoll. Her years raising two children through the Great Depression and War Years while managing a farm with her husband, Frank. Perhaps she reminisced about her once-in-a-lifetime excursion out West with Brock. Perhaps she thought about driving a calf to market in her new Oldsmobile Delta 88, or chuckling to the antics of Red Skelton. Perhaps her memories harked back to the quiet cold mornings where she and George and Phil tended to the daily ritual of drawing milk from awakening cows. Whatever recollections came to mind in those moments before her final heartbeat, it is with profound gratitude that I came to know and love her and benefit from her wonderful example.

Grandma's house on Holcroft Street in Ingersoll.

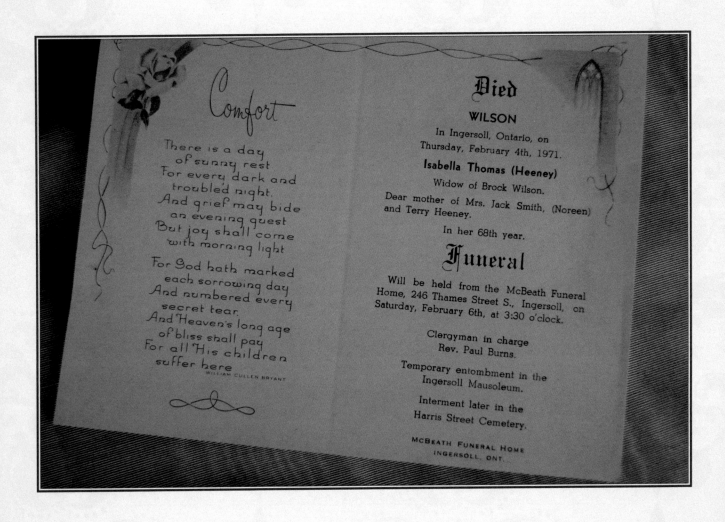

Comfort

There is a day
of sunny rest
For every dark and
troubled night.
And grief may bide
an evening guest
But joy shall come
with morning light

For God hath marked
each sorrowing day
And numbered every
secret tear
And Heaven's long age
of bliss shall pay
For all His children
suffer here
WILLIAM CULLEN BRYANT

Died

WILSON

In Ingersoll, Ontario, on
Thursday, February 4th, 1971.

Isabella Thomas (Heeney)

Widow of Brock Wilson.

Dear mother of Mrs. Jack Smith, (Noreen)
and Terry Heeney.

In her 68th year.

Funeral

Will be held from the McBeath Funeral
Home, 246 Thames Street S., Ingersoll, on
Saturday, February 6th, at 3:30 o'clock.

Clergyman in charge
Rev. Paul Burns.

Temporary entombment in the
Ingersoll Mausoleum.

Interment later in the
Harris Street Cemetery.

McBeath Funeral Home
Ingersoll, Ont.

The End

Printed in the United States
By Bookmasters